.

THE ODYSSEYS OF FALLY DOGSWELL

Originally published as
Les Odyssées de Fally Dogswell

Other works by Kelly Cogswell:
Eating Fire: My Life as a Lesbian Avenger
University of Minnesota Press, 2014

KELLY COGSWELL

THE ODYSSEYS OF FALLY DOGSWELL
words • illustrations

Translated from the French by the author

TETRAPOD

kré
kré
pek
kre
e
pte

— A. Artaud

Contents

I.
A Not At All Official Census

I lived in Paris at the time, a city of several million souls, including two million people, two hundred thousand dogs and two hundred thirty thousand cats—the lords of windowsills and crannies galore.

There were also fish. Yep. A billion of them. Plus buildings, the old ones, that had their souls, too, like the sentinels at the Luxembourg who imposed their cold and marbly weight.

I was sure that they communed. That the sober kings and queens and hunters cultivated their rage against that drunk Silène too wasted to climb on his ass and stick.

Yesterday, I went to see him by myself. Just a quarter hour. Look—some men, a nymph, the little putti dodging assly hooves. There—their flesh so tender and so hard. Silène, in his corner, doesn't give a shit about pulverized putti. And why should he? It's so peaceful near the hives and orchards. Sunny. Or not. Damp. Or not.

He dreams—that's all. He drinks. He smiles. Far from the kings that gaze at the Senate's bleached palace. Even further from the queens that surveil the overly-solemn children and their fucking boats that should sink from time to time, but persist there, on the surface of the pool.

And me, I was there, like them back in 2010. In the numbers. In the gardens. An official (human) visitor if you believe my visa's crossed words. One among two million folks. Or maybe I was only three-quarters. Like all fractured foreigners I leave trails of dust behind. From Kentucky to New York. Paris. New York. Paris. New York. Paris. You can follow if you want and collect it bit by bit. Use it to make mud. Sculpt a little figure. Breathe on the mess and wait. Look. My quarter soul's found its place.

I should introduce myself, Kelly Cogswell, nice to meet you. I know it's a rotten name to pronounce, but give it a try. Kali Gogswell. Wonderful! Now, I'm a destroying goddess and an enemy of the Lord. I kiss my girlfriend—hurricane. Each orgasm—earthquake. A murder. What power. I exalt. I'm amazed.

Or not.

2.
Modest Origins of the Volatile Kind

I was born in Kentucky. Hatched—to be precise. With this Humpty Dumptyish skull, round and bald, that was always plotting something. Nothing good. My mother sat on me for years. In the nest I made underneath her armchair, I was whole. And little. Of course I was, when I was two, three years old. I also hid in the cabinets under the kitchen sink, and sprang out, overjoyed at my mother's screams. Probably she saw me. Probably I laughed like a little nut caressing the cleaning products, or the canned goods whose edges were as smooth and round as my eggly head.

Underneath the armchair, it was those thick rubber straps that I loved. I'd pull on them just a little, slide one finger along the cushion's knobby fabric. I'll declare it blue-green, even if I'm not sure of the color any more. But the texture, yes. And the pleasure of being in a space just my size, that belonged only to me. When it was cold, there was a vent nearby that exhaled a delicious heat. I loved that, too. And shivering, put my tiny naked feet on the warming grate.

In summer, cold air emerged, and at night, my sisters and I would take turns standing over the one in the hallway. The air burst out, swoled the fabric of our nightgowns. Look, three children pregnant with cold. "It's my turn, now!" "No!" "Mom!"

My father was knocked up, too, and when he wasn't traveling, I'd stretch out on his belly and listen to his heart beat day and night like a clock. I'd practically forgotten this comfortable mound, and his pine and juniper perfume. He was an amateur photographer. Often wore yellow golf shirts. Gave birth to a bottle of gin. My obsession of stretching out on the sofa. Taking photos of pretty girls.

How sweet these memories are. So touching and cute I'm gonna puke. What are they good for, anyway? These that remain? I'll leave them with you, dear readers. Do what you like with them.

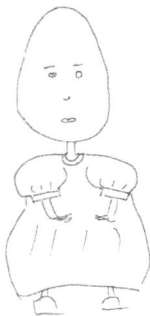

3.
In the Labyrinth

After four years in New York, we came back to Paris. I can't remember why anymore. It rains. It rains all the time. The tree across the street is getting huge. It dances. It turns. It does the twist. While me, I wait. We did an exchange. Our apartment in New York for theirs here on rue Daubenton. I already broke a bowl, burnt a pot, and scattered frozen fries all over the floor.

I'm uncomfortable. I haven't really re-entered the city. The stones, the sidewalks aren't mine anymore, reject me. I bump against the baby carriages, bang against the other pedestrians. Am covered in bruises. I step into a discount shop, but the North African owner and her black friend turn their eyes away after a glance. Maybe they're disappointed. I'm too old to be a student. So I must be poor. It's shameful. I should have done better given the advantage of this white skin.

Sorry, ladies. I embarrass my race, even here, among the other adult women of the neighborhood that are more

15

feminine, better dressed, though often in clothes full-on nun. Plain skirt, blouse, sweater. Only a scarf saves them from the convent. The store ladies take me back to the New York of the Nineties and the crappy public clinic where the employees used to silently assess me each time I went in. The only white among the black and brown crowd. Either I was a screw-up, or some kind of welfare cheat. And they'd drum on the mountains of paperwork with their long red polished nails and scream at me when I tried to go to the john. "That's the women's!" As if I were a man. A spy. A monster. These breasts not big enough. The jeans ambiguous, too.

One day, I'm gonna quit washing my cunt, and my particularly female stink will proceed me like a passport every time I have to piss. Open the door! Fuck!

If only I could remember why I returned. All the memories that drew me, all those years here, have disappeared. Poof! Rupture! Rapture! What do I do now? I can't even remember the story I was going to tell you, or why. To understand? Maybe invoke the past? Find a thread to grab? Collect the crumbs of my broken head? Or why not my neck? I'd give anything for a rope.

They're right—the screaming women. I'm capable of anything. Even the most monstrous. No, I lie. Violence, I usually save for myself. Inflict comings and goings, reproaches.

But the thread. Of Time.

16

How to find the right end after four, five years? Time's sprouted. Changed. But surely there's a loop sticking up past the surface somewhere. I'm going to look for it. I was, I am, a journalist. And afterwards... We'll see.

4.
Damn Stones!

I'll start here, in this enormous, crumbling cathedral—Saint-Germain l'Auxerrois. At least, I remember it. In front, there's a photographer and an Asian couple in fancy wedding clothes. Damn, they're fine! Maybe they're models. Maybe real lovebirds ready to consecrate their lust. Probably they don't know the place's history. The bell that rang, rang, rang to unleash the massacre of my Huguenot ancestors. Or maybe the thousands of dead give their ceremony a tasty little edge.

Dunno. I come here to think. It's not forbidden, not yet. Sitting and day-dreaming. Even in cemeteries. And here, one time, the Madonna spoke to me. I swear. The Madonna who lives in the chapel on the side. I was looking at her from behind a kind of sculpted grill. The air smelled of old wood, incense, dust. And suddenly... Well, I'll keep to myself what she said. This presence that sprang into my head. At any rate, she spoke to me. The only time in all these years that a god or their ilk took an interest in me. Young, I used to talk to them, but the conversations were all a little one-sided, of course. Like with Freudian shrinks.

Still, I felt better when I prayed. Connected to the Universe. To the world of the Spirit. Because of that, I addressed myself to God, and not Jesus. A matter of flesh. I didn't like male bodies. Even those of demi-gods with their masculinity so absolutely blatant. Poor Jesus, practically nude in his suffering that should be hidden away. My God! What will the neighbors think?

God, as for Him, He was the opposite. Omni -potent, -present. But also a great big Nothing. No body, see? So no sexual tension. I prayed. I felt a presence. That's all. I was totally hooked. A real fucking mystic. I saw God everywhere. In the leaves of trees, snowflakes. The cold. The heat. I hung out in the church. In the empty sanctuary. And floated up to God among the old wine red cushions.

Other times, I'd go to the nursery upstairs. There was a sandbox, but filled with rice. And running my hands through the smooth, cool grains, I'd compose sermons. The taste of God in my mouth. The words intended for… Who, really? My fragile, terrifying mother? The multitudes far from the joy and peace of God? I can't remember anymore. Just that I was transformed. I was strong, direct, as serious as a light saber. Not at all that ridiculous creature—a girl.

5.
The Samaritaine

Good lord, I'm tired. Not you? Not yet annoyed at my strange, broken sentences? Anyway… I go slowly into the church. No need to run like before. There are no more nets around the sculptures in front. I suppose they've been repaired. The wings of monsters stabilized as well as the heads of angels who have watched over humans for centuries. The good and the bad. The mediocre. Losing their neutrality little by little and becoming less stone than before, crumbling, even restored. At least, when they fall, it's not my problem. Not the cholera or typhoid either that you can catch from the water in the stoup. It's disgusting, that water. Rimmed by this green-brown stuff. Besides that, the church is more or less what I remember. Open and calm. Cool. Even the tourists remain respectful. Don't scream. Let the silence enter through their skin. This silence of what? Of God? Or maybe Time. Museums are the same. Like fields when night falls. Or bars still empty at 3 p.m. except for the blues streaming from the jukebox.

Once, I saw a woman enter and kneel in front of a big crucified Jesus not far from the entry. She exposed her soles. At her side, bags from the Samaritaine department store. Her head didn't move, was as immobile as that of the wooden guy who had his own concerns. For example, the nails in his hands and feet. I watched her with curiosity, and envy, too. What did she want exactly? This woman with perfect stockings and Manolo Blahnik heels. How dare she demand pity, demand help from this figure stuck there like anybody at all? Exiled from all movement, except decay? Lately, I've preferred a god a little more available. With visible resources. Like tridents. Or lightning bolts. At least a nice bottle of wine. You can drink it, laugh, dream, or smack somebody with it. They're fucking solid, these bottles.

At any rate, she left suddenly, the Samaritaine bag lady. While I, I stayed practically alone (as human) in the massive building. It was a big Buddha, present and calm, serene. With no intention of moving come what may. The Cloisters museum, there in New York, is beautiful, but leaves a different impression. Its spirit seems disturbed, divided, probably because its stones, its feet were ripped from several places. Nobody asked, You wanna come or what? Or do you want to stay here, crumble bit by bit? Become dust, mud again? Rejoin the earth after centuries apart?

Not everybody's obliged to be useful. Stay standing. Move. Even if you've heard the voice of the Virgin in your head. Even if the bitch said, "Persevere."

nuestra señora de
petits chats

where's Peaseblossom?

6.
Bad Words

I'm sitting at a café with Marina. At least there's that. Behind us, a group of women. They're regulars, get so much pleasure out of their little cups of coffee and ever so leisurely conversation. They laugh. I understand everything they're saying. I'm comfortable—for the moment—there in the sun. Surrounded by these songs of human sounds. I want to speak, too, but don't dare open my mouth. What will come out? Braying and meows? I'm afraid of saying something stupid, getting humiliated. Remaining a foreigner. In foreign parts you have to be stronger than you know. Even if you don't screw up, you're marked, set apart. Your accent emerges. Your sad mug. I, who wanted to be lost in god, I feel so big, swollen, in fact, with your ideas and my own fear.

Back home, I take this notebook, write. Which is even more perilous. I approach your language, it retreats. I approach, it breaks, scatters shards. Before, it was as whole as water. So, why write with this hammer, this knife? I destroy, I discover. Look! I am there. In places that are unexpected, inaccessible in my own language which flows. Somebody at least gets there. Not really "I." Who flees all the time. Leaves behind her another "I." A little empty, without history or tongue. Memories don't travel from one language to another. There's no way to translate those words that are found in this human purgatory of the half-forgotten.

The worst this time is that. The amnesia. The discontinuities. I have enormous gaps. As if my head had been struck by a hammer. Or as if I fell from a wall. Suffering ruptures not at all foreseen by Mr. Plato and his bits of humans that need each other to re-become circular beings, complete. Of what are we made? And me, even twinned with Marina, I barely walk, don't do cartwheels.

The first time in Paris was different. Marina and I arrived on the run, expecting nothing. I barely knew five words in French. In the beginning I floated. Practically like a newborn, nude in this place without language, without a history for me. Gone—George W. Bush, and Guantanamo. The Iraq war. Torture. Echoes. I should have known. I felt as light as I did when I left Kentucky with a hundred bucks and one sad suitcase. It was 1989. I'd gotten a spot in a graduate program in New York. I travelled by bus. I like the bus. The relationship made visible between space and time. The comfort of movement.

But I quickly discovered that there is a wall, a frontier somewhere that you can't cross without being terribly freed of everything, even yourself.

why do they run Away?

7.
Eden

If only I hadn't said that word, *lesbian*, maybe I would have had it, the right of return. But nope. Soon after I got to New York, I wrote it to my mother. A fragile, religious, bitter woman. Already shocked by my sisters' blue eye-shadow. Revolted by my brief life as a goth. And her, when she read that cursed word in a letter, she banished me. Her youngest daughter. Her little bird. She should have known it already. Me, too, by the way. I, who never had a boyfriend. Few dates. Not that many friends even, male or female. Except for that first year of high school when I met a girl in the Louisville Youth Orchestra who also played field hockey like me.

She had short curly hair, incredibly white skin with freckles on her open face. She laughed at my jokes, admired my poems. Together, we exchanged painful histories of painful mothers. Went for drives in her grandmother's car. See-sawed on the see-saw. Played in the creek not long from the practice fields in a park. It was surrounded by trees, with miraculous leaves that fell into the water and danced like little boats. That creek was so cold. Once, during an enormous storm, we threw ourselves in and floated practically half a mile. Afterwards, we stuffed ourselves with a bunch of sacramental Oreos.

I even took her to church. Not long afterwards she got baptized. Saved from God knows what because of me. Even if we'd had all of Nature to ourselves.

I'm so sorry. I apologize. My beautiful…

I don't dare write her name. Because of that, maybe. To have put her in the big hands of Brother Storment who dipped her into water so far from the creek. Or maybe because I loved her. And to love without knowing seems pitiful, shameful even. Yeah, I'm ashamed to have been so blind. To have noticed nothing. Me who was top of the class in Spanish and in English. Who knew all those bible verses by heart. But that…

Poor little chick. To keep mum, she (a previous "me") must have been so afraid.

I wonder if she knew I loved her. That girl with watery blue eyes and little freckles. She was three years older than me. She who presented herself in front of me not long ago with a strange and hesitant smile. I was in Kentucky as a New York, dyke writer. Trapped in a bookstore. "Remember me?"

No, actually. Until that moment I'd forgotten her. Go back where you came from. Go!

8.
Drag

May the wind take them. The fluff of dandelions. Memories. May they rot. May they burn. What they are really—memories? Repeated words? Photos? Scars? I arrived in New York with nearly empty hands. Just two or three already yellowed snaps. In one of them, my sisters and I are on the couch, and I'm a fat little baby in a Santa suit. In another, taken at school, I'm missing a bunch of teeth. And my mother, when I asked her later for more pics, actually agreed. Sent me two or three photos taken at the prom. I seemed so feminine, was practically in drag. Permanented hair in curls. Made up face. As accessory—a guy. And this incredible dress.

I'd almost forgotten that dress. It was so beautiful. In silk, I think, sea green and so smooth. Tight on top and through the waist. Then cascading all the way to my feet. It was my mother's. She wore it as bridesmaid for god knows who. I was so proud to put it on. I hadn't

31

understood, not yet, dresses' deceptive cries, "I'm available." "I'm normal." "I am… yours." Fucking photos. My mother sent them along with the marriage announcements of my childhood friends. They were reproaches. Shards of glass.

She wanted to wound, erase, annihilate me. After my "coming out," when she banished me in the name of God, she threw out my clothes, sold my violin. As for my letters… Last year, when she returned several packets of things to my sisters. Letters and postcards sent from Girl Scout camps, from college. I discovered she had nothing of mine, even from those distant years in New York. And I imagined her with these papers in her hand and a match. Then, I wondered what young Kelly could have written. What would she have wanted to share with her mother? Or maybe hide. Nobody knows. Even me.

At least I was an adult when my mother flipped out, cut all ties. Everywhere, you see these lost, dazed children, tossed in the street by their families. Poor kids, who form tribes, tattoo, pierce themselves. Who sell the only thing that they have.

9.
Memory Hooks

Even for me, what's left, decades afterwards, but a terrible lightness? Depths of rage and of grief? My skin? Inside, a bunch of flesh and blood, bones, a voice. I take up space with it. In the métro, my elbows say, "What the fuck are you doing? Shit. That's my spot, asshole." Or maybe I walk. I trail through the streets with my old shoes. This notebook. Wide-open eyes. With each step I caress the city. The asphalt. Stones. In Paris, the stones are luminous and white. Or brown and as full of holes as gruyère.

There's nothing but that, the solid and eternal city. She loves me. Is my Savior.

No! This time I've discovered that the streets, and buildings, the incredibly white rocks are not eternal. Or sure. They're fakers. Are vulnerable. Hide. When I'm not watching them, they move millimeter by millimeter. Go a little forward, a little back. Have sentiments and resentments. The bakery on rue Monge wasn't happy. The owners were weird; the baguettes came twisted out of the oven. I wasn't surprised when the place caught fire. On the sidewalk, there's nothing left but stains of a huge black river.

Sometimes, I'm so afraid of dissolving. Kentucky is where? Is what? A land of hillbillies? Or fried chicken? Horses, right? Even me, I've forgotten. My memories have disappeared, flown off, and the creek girl with them. In Lexington, once, I had a drink with a couple of old college friends. They told stories that were so funny we laughed all afternoon. Except that I didn't remember anything. Not the time our car caught fire at a gas station. (How things love to burn!) Or when I had to help one of them mugged practically at my doorstep. Brave girl, she chased the fucker down the street to get her bag back.

They were all so beautiful these girls, these women. Their memories to hand like smokes. In their mouths, the same language pronounced with the same accent. In their bags, their wallets full of snaps. Each familiar thing is a hook, a trap. Without them, history evaporates. And us with it.

I eat the smells of the city, its sounds. Like ballast. With the cries of the crows, sparrows, bells, I take on weight, take up space again. Dogs water each corner, each tree. I imagine that I also leave my trace like them.

Except… No. Something's coming back. It's 1990. The summer. I'd only been in New York a year, had a little studio on Grand Street. A cat. Alice B. Toklas Scaredy-cat. And my first openly lesbian lover. I'd written to my mother to tell her I was happy with Amy. And when she informed me she was washing her hands of me, she returned all the letters and cards I'd ever sent her like a rejected mistress. And me, when I saw my childish handwriting, the little packets tied up with faded ribbons, I was stunned. I imagined a bridge and I burnt it. And in five minutes, 24 years of memories, maybe more, disappeared.

10.
Mother Minotauros

I return to the Paris rain, and the present, 2014, take a quick glance at social media, and find a post by my sister. Something's the matter with my mother. I call her. She's fallen again, and anyway is practically a skeleton now. She doesn't eat. Imagines it's already been done, this thing of lunch, dinner. "I don't want to gain weight," she laughs. "Like your disgusting father. Your sister." So she finds herself in a nursing home with strange walls. At least for the moment. She's afraid. Can't remain alone at home. Doesn't want to have a companion. Even less to move. "Oh no. Not that. Impossible."

She knows full well that leaving 3333 Cornelia Drive won't make an Odysseus of her. No one returns from this voyage. There's only one more adventure. Death. Leaving her home would be an admission. Even I feel pity for her. She who doesn't want to die. Me either. Except those days when I want to be already dead. At least asleep. Or drunk. The uncertainty of life is too much. I can't stand it anymore.

It's August. When's the last time I saw her—my mother? In April, I think. Before that it had been fifteen years since I'd seen her. I was afraid. Me. All grown up. Even if she'd softened a little, decided she could talk to me without destroying her soul or mine. For decades, I'd imagined her a monster. A Minotaur. With reason. You can lose yourself around her. Be horribly hurt. She likes a nice bloody sacrifice. And me, I'm a real coward. I confess. So, I asked a friend, Adrienne, to go with me. Be the thread Ariane gave Odysseus. "Don't go so fast," I beg her on the way. She laughs. We went by our old high school, ugly and poor. The tiny yards of tiny houses. The trees had grown a lot. Except at home. I find that my mother had gotten most of them cut down. The maple, the dogwood, the crabapple. She replaced them with grass and flowers. No leaves in autumn, no messy fruit falling all over the place.

When we arrived, I paused so long on the driveway, that passage between the present and the past, that my mother came out of the house. And beckoned us in.

Now, it's her looking for threads. Who's afraid. Her body itself is disappearing. She'll be a bone in the desert. A bit of dust. Then—nothing.

11.
The Appearance of Things

No. Wait. I'm going too fast. Mom's not dead, not to-day. How was she when I visited in April? We all went in the house. She'd painted the walls in vibrant colors. Cobalt. Apple green. Had hung her own paintings. "I'm a real Grandma Moses," she said standing in front of the old furniture, the sofa, my beloved armchair, not at all changed. She looked just like herself, too. The same naturally red hair. The same eyes, brown and too-bright, though surrounded by wrinkles. She wore jeans, and two sweaters because she was already too thin and felt cold. And she smiled. Yes, how she smiled. Way too much, like me. And she laughed, too. Was nervous. Was afraid. Of me. It was Adrienne who told me afterwards. I'd only noticed that she wasn't mean to me. In fact, she wanted me to stay, spend the night there, in her house. What a terrifying idea. Trapped there, the memories, where the "I" yo-yos between the me of four years, twelve, almost fifty years old. I suppose she forgot I was a disgusting dyke. She, who never pronounced the name of my girlfriend of two decades, Marina. Marina.

Still, I was moved to hug her for the first time in thirty years. Her shoulders were so boney. And she, so grateful.

I should have felt victorious, right? At least indifferent. But we also mourn our fallen enemies. Even if they're frail. And it's been years that I abandoned that battlefield, the wounds, vengeance, armor, too. I'm a little shellless larva. I let my enemies attack right at my heart. My voice is often theirs. Sometimes, even my eyes belong to them, and in the mirror I find myself ugly. I'm too fat. My clothes don't suit me. I have no grace when I move. Probably, I stink. I never wanted to be het, but I fall short even as a dyke. I make people scream. Am ridiculous.

Nevertheless, every once in a while I see the reflection of a girl in the window of the métro, and I find her—handsome. It's so shocking to see that dyke there. Her (my) profile attracts me. It is immobile. It says something. Behind the calm, there's a sadness. And behind that, practically unnoticed, there's maybe joy. I want to say, "Wake up. Do something! Be light again. Or heavy. Be as heavy as a stone." But how? I'm not zen enough to become either stone or water. One day, I'll become pure dust, like everyone else. Or maybe a fish.

12.
Proust At the Pool

Today, I go to the pool at the worst possible time. Just when people leave their jobs and play at being fishes, trying to avoid each other in the water at noon.

I hit a bunch. And they hit me. "Sorry, uh. Shit."

Still, it is nice.

We all go into the same dressing rooms, man, woman, dyke. I unwind in the water. I truly float. Sounds come from far away. But are clear. Ideas, too, are more precise. They don't get mixed up with the sounds of traffic, the neighbor's TV. The fucking pigeons. I would like to be a whale. They make music. Sing with deep and mysterious voices. They take up space.

Afterwards, I'm famished. I buy a baguette at the corner, eat a bit. I imagine there's a name for that tiny little nub at the end, but I don't know what it is. At any rate, it doesn't exist anymore. It's in my mouth, then my belly. I'll make a sandwich for two. Something enormous. At home, I cut cheese, cucumber, tomato, onion, avocado. Stick it into strata. Can't close the thing. But it won't escape. I cut it in two, put it on a plate, and voilà. Lunch!

I stop in mid-chew. Something else is coming back. I remember... shit. My mother again. I'm little. She's standing in the kitchen with its very yellow walls. With something in her hand. Something I've never seen. That she's eating with a spoon. But it's not ice cream, even if she seems so delighted that I ask for a bite. She explains that it's something hard to get and really expensive. I insist. Unfortunately, she gives in. I put it in my mouth. My god how avocado is disgusting. Green and slimy. "It must be rotten," I say. "That's it."

My mother thinks I'm hilarious. She laughs. Hugs me.

It's been about twenty, thirty years since I've seen that open smile. So, let us mourn as well the fleeting woman who was audacious, happy, indulgent, generous. Open to pleasure. And longtime dead. No, stop! Chill out. Shit.

13.
Luco

Still, there're advantages to being nude in the world. Light. You can stroll slowly. Discover a bunch of things. If you lack memories, you can always steal someone else's. Or invent them. Grab the little ones and inflate them. Yesterday evening, we were at the Pantheon to watch the Bastille Day fireworks. There were a lot of young people. Each with their bottle of rosé and an ironic smile. They weren't blind patriots, not them. But a picnic is always nice. And finally, they shouted with astonishment and joy after each explosion.

While we were waiting, we sat on the cold, dirty paving stones. Behind us was the vast dome, and the bones of dead guys plus Marie Curie. In front, the shining streets of the city. Nearby, a woman and her small son. When latecomers tried to keep standing up, she opened her big mouth and screamed, "Sit down!" with such authority that everyone fell immediately to the ground and stayed there. Even if she had an American accent that was even worse than mine. I admired her, looked at her for a long time.

Today, I went to the Luco, and she was there too, this woman of the wide-opened mouth who was at home everywhere. She recognized me and smiled. But we didn't say anything. The sun shone and not the moon. Nothing exploded. I passed the lion with his prey and came to the orchard. Carefully examined the pear and apple trees. Then my beloved persimmon where the little balls of fruit were starting to appear. Further along, the bees buzzed Bizet's big opera.

I was waiting for the moment when I'd be like that woman, entirely at ease. I no longer wanted to be an observer of the landscape, but inside it, a citizen, of the city at least. I wouldn't need to laugh all the time, or smile. To do anything at all. Just breathe. Be alive. I let my eyes slide this way, then that. I was looking for a hole where I could hide and rest. I wanted to be a bench. A tree. A pigeon. Even if I don't like pigeons. Last time in Paris I became a statue. Maybe that's the story I wanted to tell you. A woman changed into a sphinx. Yeah. Made of paper and flesh. I'm not kidding. There's even a video.

14.
The Sphinx

Everybody has obsessions, even the poor. They don't take up much space, ideas. You can put several in the same suitcase. Thousands, actually. Or one big one. Mine appeared after a visit to Versailles during our last trip. We saw the enormous castle. The grounds. The little village where the queen had her own manias. I loved the palace decor, especially the stuff inspired by Egypt and Greece. The extraordinary colors. The sculptures. Above all, the sphinx.

The creature followed me, grew, multiplied itself. This astonishing being with wings, little lion feet, tits. Often the girls (I insist on the sex) are forced to hold up tables or walls. But they're not upset. Not much. They wait. They always wait with the dignity of those who are fierce but constrained. By the rules of the game. Or by their material which is so hard. At any rate, they're far-removed from us, we humans. Maybe their fight is on another plane. Or they're amused to pose. All cats are jokers. They even play with their unfortunate prey. I shouldn't forget either that sphinx guard the road. Ask riddles. You have to find the right response to get by. Answer wrong, it's death. Or worse, you're stuck there at the crossroads.

I found them in the city, statues of sphinx. In front of some quai. Then a building. Two. Three. Shit. A little everywhere. With echoes in the wings of pigeons. Of angels. I wanted to see even more, these monstrous figures. Masculine and feminine. Of lion and eagle. Of stone. Immobile. In a state of refusal. I imagined above all their haunches in empty spaces. Parks. Roofs. I wanted to become a sphinx. I did.

I made wings with plastic tubes. With string. Sheets of paper ripped from a book, page by page, a biography of that asshole Che Guevara, yeah, him. The architect of Cuban gulags for whores, an assortment of Christians, and homos of course. Our bodies, our lives so subversive that we were much more than sinners, but enemies of the heterophile homo-dox Cuban state. My girlfriend among them. Her friends. Those that tasted the work camps, the jails. The doctors' tortures. Here, there're no political prisoners, they said to Marina just before the electroshocks.

I did a test as a sphinx at home dressed only in a bra and underpants. You have to expose yourself. Pursue immobility, too. I did my best. It wasn't easy. Too much pressure on my knees. And the wings were beautiful, but hard to hold. How exactly did I feel, besides stupid and uncomfortable? Practically nude on the table. A video camera the only eye? I admit it. I felt good, too. I managed to switch roles. I wasn't the suppliant at the crossroads anymore, but the beast. I escaped my life, my body. For an instant. Right away I wanted to repeat it. Put myself in empty spaces, in public places that desperately needed a statue. A being half-sphinx, half dyke.

Afterwards, everything was different. I resumed my trajectory as an artist that had long been abandoned. And I found my place in Paris after five years there. When I was forced to leave just two months later, I was destroyed, exiled again. Poor fucker weeping at a Whole Foods market in New York.

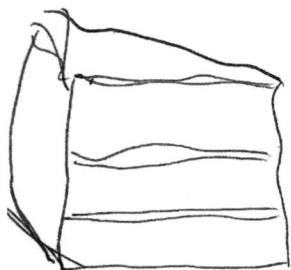

This is
my body

Ceci
est mon
corps

15.
Marriage, Rue des Martyrs

That seems so distant. I was someone else. You, too. Or not.

At St. Jean's church in Montmartre, I watch a woman polish the enormous candlesticks, and other altar baubles. She's fiftyish. Is concentrated on her task. I imagine she's not paid but does it as a gesture of devotion. Of hope. Like me, I go to demos. I write bimonthly articles for a gay rag. Demand equality. Justice. Freedom. What a joke.

At any rate, the church is clean, the stained glass nice. It's really calm, even with the guitarist outside in the Place des Abbesses who wants to be Jimi Hendrix. It intrigues me, this church. Maybe because it's relatively modern. We don't build them anymore these days, except in the United States where mega-idiocies take their place among the enormous factories and produce just as much dough, and two times more hate. My sister who stayed in Kentucky goes to one that denounces the Gays, and doesn't let women preach. The female mouth dirties up the words. Leaves them polluted.

The Catholic church in France is no better. But their buildings are open at least. Often used for concerts and other city happenings. Here, at Place des Abbesses, the Church has lost the battle, and also the war. At least, I hope. During the day, anybody at all can enter. Today, I came to rest my feet. I admire the floor. It's not of stone, but of wood laid down in a herringbone pattern. Then, I look at the center aisle where there's sometimes a priest, sometimes a bride, and for the first time in my life I try to imagine myself there. Bad idea. I immediately feel sick, practically faint.

Invite people to do what? Stare at us? Offer their support? Presents? I love presents. We need a good toaster. And dressed in what? My closet's empty. It's a mystery. Such an intimate thing. Marriage. Here? In front of everyone. Even a tortured Jesus? How weird. And yet, and yet. I should be able to imagine anything. I myself fought for the right. The act of imagining the ceremony shouldn't be so violent.

Two girls in the aisle, one of them me—inconceivable.

Even if I saw a dyke wedding at City Hall in New York. The parents of one girl with tears in their eyes. The mostly feminist crowd striking ironic poses. Mandatory for the photos of this ultra heteronormative act by two activist lesbians. One bride was happy. The other practically nuts with joy. After all, she worked a lot in Nigeria. Had gay friends targeted, killed even as devils, traitors, foreigners. She's been attacked herself. So... What happiness, what joy to be transformed into a human being, a citizen, with these simple sacraments of cake and champagne. I love you.

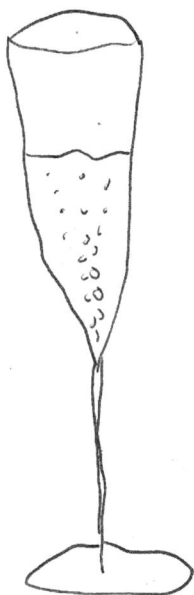

Buvez-en
tous

16.
Thug Dyke

I have other things on my lips. Blood and flesh. Words. Now, a little speech about joy. The joy of evil. Of violence. Inspiring hate and fear. And not only in my mother. I tasted it that time I was a newborn lesbian activist with a leather jacket and shaved head. It was in 1994 at the corner of First and First in New York where the cars had nearly killed me a million times. That night I'd had enough. I stopped dead in the middle of the street, and banged on a hood of a car and screamed. The people inside were terrified. And I was so happy. Great! I thought. They deserved it. How many times have they terrorized me, these big guys with or without some wheels. But not this time. This time it's me the alpha wolf who bears her teeth and howls.

You gotta admit it. It's less and less hidden, our capacity for violence and hate. It takes root online. Then explodes in the streets. In the ultra-political landscape.

That night I learned it's way nicer to be the attacker than the attacked. I, too, have borders that you shouldn't cross. What joy to see their gaping mouths, their bulging eyes. What power. What a temptation. Imagine! To be done with persuasion, reason, supplication, words. The little lezzy demos where you're supposed to soften anger with humor because we're women and you have to say everything with a pretty smile. Yeah, to be done with all that. Have things immediately. To force. To terrorize. I've surely got the right after all I've lived through.

Yeah, what a delight. The taste of others' fear. How humiliating to show it. To feel so satisfied. To take pleasure. Like you. My mother full of rage, of violence of her kind. She'd hit us with whatever was at hand, a wooden spoon, a fly swatter. But she preferred words as a weapon. Reducing you to nothing. She'd scream with fury and with hate. You're dirty. You stink. You're no good like your father.

For years, even in my nightmares, we fought like two demons. She'd grab me. And me, I'd try to escape. Finally, I'd bite off a finger and she'd let go. Her bloody finger in my mouth. I was a rabid dog, a maenad. Now, I've only got words in my mouth. Even in my dreams, I discuss. I dispute with everyone. Vomit a river of blab and wake all dry. Maybe I leave a ravine, a gully somewhere.

Because I know that this violence is there in me, I watch myself carefully. Often I make myself small, too small, practically cute. I don't wear a leather jacket anymore. After a day in front of the computer, I don't even have a body. But not you. So be warned.

Regarde
comme
mon
épée
est
GRANDE

I'm no pussy fisherman

17.
Archeology Above All

At the Carnavalet museum, they have bits of wooden canoes. Utensils. Some fired clay pots from the Parisii fisherman installed on the right bank—debris left by the very first Parisians. I imagine them as peaceful, patient, vulnerable, and as screwed as me faced with the very imperial Romans who took their place and built this beautiful Lutetia with its baths, its characteristic arenas. The bones of one of them is two minutes from here, on rue Monge. I play boules there with a friend. Nobody dies. The 14th of July or the 13th the firemen put up a stage, and hold an inundated dance.

With the river and the rain it's hard to ignore water here. Simple to imagine fishermen in their canoes. We were at the Jardin des Plantes, yesterday, when a big storm left us soaked. A thoroughly drenched life, that's one thread, at least, between me and the fisherfolk of times gone by. Everybody tries to make connections. Or tries to destroy them. I imagine my poor Huguenot cousins. My nest under the Kentucky armchair. Its rough, blue-green cushion.

In front of the garden is the Buffon library that I often visit. Its windows look out on the trees and the carrousel. I like watching it. Hearing the children scream like seagulls that find refuge here, too, in this watery city.

To the side, in the windows of the Natural History Museum, you can see skeletons that look like giant lizards. I suppose they belonged to dinosaurs. A few have, or had, wings. They're the great-great-great-great (et cetera) grandparents of flying children. Is it Time itself that fascinates, that scares us? Or this ancestral connection?

Dunno. I look. I look at the children who sprout everywhere in this country, far more than the rest of Europe. Maybe when you play a stone's throw from skeletons. From memento mori. Total extinction. Reproducing yourself becomes obligatory. Especially if you believe that human beings should move all the time. Shouldn't keep silent inside stone inside bones. We lose nothing but energy. And even that's up for debate.

18.
Flea Circus

In the U.S., people are in the streets. Another black man was shot by a white cop. Killed also, but without demos, another fag. I don't know who did it. I make my token gesture. Write an article for both. Try to say something that's worth the trouble. About hate. The necessary social change. I cry, "Justice." I cry, "Rage." But against what? Or whom? The killers? The system which encourages them? Churches? Cynical politicians on all sides, right and left?

You need to distract people? There's always a Jew, a Homo. A Black.

I cry the words that I've cried a thousand times. In English, words don't hide. They demand their space. Come in drips or in floods. But are dead. I've lost my faith. Words don't bring anybody back. Things change, sure, but gains are fragile. And Michael Brown. Bryan Higgins. They stay dead.

In this notebook, French words mean other things. Are not unfindable, but don't sing, don't flow. Aren't water, but pebbles that come by the fistful. Have limits. Are like sonnets with their obligatory structures there behind each line. That take time. You're forced to be more creative. But that's the point.

At any rate, it's not real to write in French. In France. I can say whatever nonsense I want. Play. Dare. Consider things obliquely. Here, I'm nothing, this American dyke of considerable foreignness but no authority at all. It doesn't matter. I jump. I bite like a little flea. And this circus is entirely mine. I'm free. At least in my head. At least, sometimes. In the street I'm still a female body. Targeted. Never at home.

Sunday, we went to the Bastille market taking Henri IV boulevard where we stopped to take a look at Barye park. Nice. Even if, in this city of free public toilets, there was a man behind the pines in the back who was in the middle of, maybe, pissing. A woman entered after us all by herself. Took a couple steps towards the guy half-hidden from view. Didn't see the man who watched her. Or didn't notice she was trapped between the pines and the railing.

Of course we stayed, to observe. The man was annoyed, poor fuck with his dick in his hand. He glared at us. Nobody really likes fleas. Are ready to destroy them at any moment. Even if they take up so little room.

They bother me, too, these little beasts. Moving here, moving there. Their power in this ability. To run around freely, in their vulnerable state, to bother. Force you to do things. To poison yourself with anti-insect bombs, for example. Even under attack, fleas don't flee, they hide somewhere, in the apartment next door. Or in the little—and largely indifferent—cracks of your own gleaming floor.

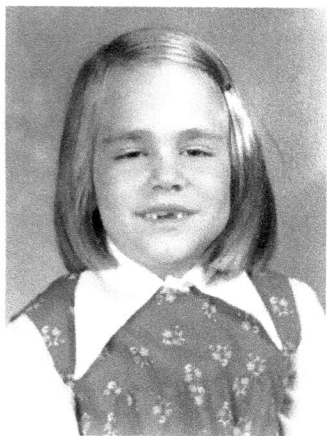

19.
The War of the Worlds

Me, I have my own war. Against the world of Things. Today's enemy—a broken little blue glass barrette. I admit that I tried to toss it on the dresser. But it didn't want to stay. From the beginning it didn't like me. Maybe because I found it ridiculous. This thing with its tiny cartoon flowers. It was Marina's mom who gave it to me after a trip to Italy when I managed not to kill her. For real? You want me to put *that* in my hair?

I said, "Thanks," anyway, and tossed it in a drawer somewhere. It hated the dark. And being forgotten. Found me stupid, more rigid than it. Insipid, dour, even misogynistic. It mocked me, "You think you're so naked and open. But open to what, exactly, my little dykelette?" That reminded me of my father. Once, for my birthday, he gave me gold earrings. I had ears, but no little holes. Nor the desire, by the way, to wear them. Besides, I'd spent months dropping hints that I wanted a field hockey stick.

I was the goalie of my high school team. I needed it. And when I opened this little, delicate box, I was shocked by these two things that were practically extraterrestrial... so terribly, so obligatorily... feminine. To get revenge, I did the same. For his birthday, I gave him enormous pink plastic earrings. And he and his new wife tried to laugh.

I got my ears pierced later, but the earrings knew I'd rejected the others. They lost themselves. The holes themselves didn't want to stay open. Or maybe my body decided it should get rid of everything but the most essential. The rest is borrowed. Even my name. Kayee Bogswell.

Then one day, about a year ago, I opened the drawer and felt almost tender towards the little ridiculous barrette. And I put it in my hair for months. It made me seem lighter. Like that pink leather bomber hat that I wear sometimes with my black coat and my German army pants. It's a sign of the contradictions of the genre of gender. Nobody's entirely masculine or feminine. Or even mammal. I'd say mineral's more likely for me. I rejoice in the strata. In unexpected mixes. The leaf and the little bones petrified in the mud. The dry river. The dust. Yes, the layers of sublime and eternal dust which become rock. And the stones of the pyramid. And the sphinx. Resist. Resist.

20.
Zombies

And yet, and yet. She's old, my mother. This world. She's beside herself now. Doesn't remember anything. She asks everybody just what she did to be abandoned. I shouldn't call her. I should do it immediately. When I rang the other day she asked, "Where are you? Paris? Oooh-la-la." She was delighted, said, "I'm going to tell everyone that my daughter called me from Paris." It's the least I can do—call from Paris. She's so old. I don't do it. There are postcards in my notebook. I bought them for her. I leave them tucked inside.

I go to the window, stand there, look. The sun shines for the first time today. It's pure deceit. Most of the sky is the same color as the slate roofs. I admire the black stains above the pale yellow buildings. People come out of metro holes like little bees. Ah. This neighborhood is inhabited. I'd started to wonder.

Still, I can practically see her. Sitting, she pushes her red hair back with a bony hand. She smiles like a child.

Is practically flirtatious with the nurses' aides who help her get dressed and eat and bathe. It says, this smile, "Love me." But then, she opens her mouth and lets the poison out. I wonder if they laugh, these certainly black nursing aides. If they are nice, equally smiling in the face of this little aging and vulnerable monster who, even bare-assed, will explain how she's not racist. There are good blacks. She herself had a black friend, so intelligent and clean. And not at all violent.

Or maybe she'll attack herself. "I'm dense, stupid, clumsy, worthless. Why hasn't God taken me? Why?"

Shit. Even at a distance, I have her voice in my head. Am sure that I too am stupid and that the effort to express myself in any language at all, is totally idiotic. I'm garbage, and probably, yes, I stink. I didn't take a shower this morning. And besides, I'm fat and ugly. I walk all the time. I swim, but I'm getting fat. It's the season, anyway. Practically autumn and harvest time. Sycamore leaves are on the sidewalk. And what if I eat some pastry nuns. If I rip their heads off, lick their little necks. Suck their creamy stomachs out. Then I'll get fat. Be all ready for the slaughter.

And yet, and yet. I'll squeal, this piggie, until the last second.

How her accusing voice annoys me. Is as persistant as the image of beret-headed Che with his beard and raised fist. Poor fuck reduced these days to a tee-shirt life, a living death, his hate resuscitated from time to time like disco. Yes, the melodies are catchy. But careful,

John Travolta's not handsome anymore. Or thin. Or cool. His charming smile is rather false. Better watch out. It's all mine, the mud, the slime. The raucous sounds. The dirty claws of the sphinx-hog. The conquering stench.

The other night I had this dream. About zombies. Really. Thankfully, they didn't run very fast with their rotten legs. And by chance I put on a little patchouli oil. And I discovered that it was a better repellant than water from any church. Yes. I swear it. On my mother's head. Cover yourself in this disgusting stuff and you're saved.

¡Que viva Guanahacabibes!
Le travail fera de vous des hommes!

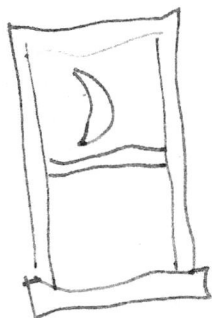

21.
Reverie, Cincy

Another tip. Don't sleep under the light of the moon unless you're looking for lunacy. Me, I've done it, obviously. More than once. Especially on my luminous mattress in Cincinnati. I lived there a year after I graduated from college. One night, I hung out in a tree hollow from bottom to top. It was like a cannon waiting for a cannonball—the moon over my head. In my arboreal nest, I wasn't afraid of spiders. Or promenading men.

Not too much, anyway. There, in the dark, in the night, the tree, I was looking for something. Maybe the moon, or death. Maybe love. I was a little suicidal that year. Put myself in danger. Abandoned myself to the flow. And to poetry. I had no goal. Or country. Or people. Just a certain emerging knowledge. If I'd been a fag, I would for sure have fucked everybody sans rubber in public johns. But I was a dyke. Practically. And I didn't know how to find others like me. And for months I didn't try to touch another human. Except one.

She was a painter. A real one. With two little birds. Long story, I knew her sister. Short version. We became friends. Sometimes, she sketched me, took her charcoal and traced my face, my eyes, my lips, my ears, my neck and the poor arms hidden in my enormous shirts. She drew me and then, rubbed her fingers through the dust to create volumes, shadows, flesh. Then she cooked spaghetti. And we ate, drank, maybe, a beer, or a glass of wine.

And I felt something. This terrible nameless emptiness. Sometimes, I stayed over at her place. One night, beside her in her bed, I pretended to sleep. I turned over. Put my leg over hers. And then, after a moment, pulled it back. Nobody has ever been as immobile as her. So silent and distant. She didn't say anything the following day. Me, either. We continued as before. She had a boyfriend, though I knew, once, she'd dated a girl. She read Kathy Acker, *Blood and Guts in High School*.

She introduced me to her friends. Was so free with her little birds that she let them fly and shit everywhere. They built their nests with her long blond hairs as pale as the moon. One day, she came back from her studio and discovered one of the poor little things hanging dead in her locks.

22.
Jardin des Plantes

Here, again, among the paths, the sand, the plants with their little touching labels that indicate all their known names in Latin and French. Their country of origin, too, of course. Like passports. I'm always impressed by this French mania of knowing everything. Of putting everything in order (and then breaking it). And like always, after five minutes, I'm annoyed. It's a party with ten million guests. Each with their first and last name. "Pleased to meet you." Shit. "Who are you? I've already forgotten." Better to hang out elsewhere where the plants aren't individuals. And there's just this undifferentiated green, and they're all unknown strangers.

There are crows here, too, on the paths. I don't like the French name, *corbeau*. They're beaux (beautiful), of course, up until the moment they open their beaks and do their croaks and caws. But their faces are terrifying. Have

you ever looked right in their eyes? They're so stern. Like the people at Immigration. Or Spanish priests. They remember everything. Better not be mean to them. I warn you. The discordant *crow* in English suits them better.

I like them anyway. They hop. They run with their two little legs. They take themselves seriously. The fucker on the corner never asks them, "Why aren't you smiling? Do it, now, for me." They aren't grateful for crumbs, either. It's natural to feed the hungry. Even the chic. All in black, they're ready for anything. A party. Funerals. God knows what they get up to all alone in the garden when the gates close. Do they sleep? Never. They summon. Issue verdicts. Plot. I salute them. "Good morning, Mr. Crow." And, "How are you, Madame?" They listen. They talk from time to time—crows. And one day they'll answer me. I'm sure.

We finally get to the little kitchen garden, and my joy surprises me. Even without labels, I recognize the plants. Am comforted in front of the tomatoes, yes, and zucchini, peppers. Fennel. Corn. I know all the names in French. I put down roots. Want to stay there. With my friends. Where I'm recognized. But we leave.

23.
Saint Jacques

I always leave. All the time, I'm en route. For years, I wanted to go to Compostela. A pilgrimage with a goal at least. The comfort of wedding myself to movement, accepting it. Not pretending to be at home. You walk, that's it. You walk, eat, sleep. Period. I bought maps. Books. Hiking boots that I still have. Stasis is unknown to me. At the level of dust, I'm sure that my lost particles often try to reunite. They move. Call to each other. Embrace. Demand the hat and the staff, the shell. That's nostalgia. That's grief. Do you love me?

Our first time here, I went to look at him, at the top of his tower. He was in his pilgrim's getup, and was half-covered by scaffolding. I paid my respects. I wrote him poems. Imagined his view. The changes. A long time ago, he had a church all to himself, Saint-Jacques-de-la-Boucherie, that the butchers paid for. Entrails for an altar. Kidneys for the door. Like ribs, the church was sold stone

73

by stone after the revolution. I imagine they're scattered everywhere now. Poor Saint Jacques. All that's left is one tower and his statue exposed to everyone at all with his long, outdated coat, and enormous hat.

I wonder if he misses them, the butchers with their bloody blouses. Or his life before in Spain—bloody, too. A fisherman like the Parisii, the son of Zebedee was transformed into Santiago Matamoros, John the Moor-killer, patron saint of Christians faced with Moorish infidels. I imagine he guided El Cid, Rodrigo Diaz de Vivar, another Spanish hero, who got banished too, after an impressive career, too impressive, as the defender of the faith and some king or other. There's always a king. A prince. His wife, during all this, stuck in a convent. What else could he do but become a mercenary? He worked for a Muslim nobleman. Then more Christians. A sword always finds blood.

The wife was called Jimena, and didn't stay in the convent, just for your information.

Santiago, as for him, mellowed after a while. Like me. Abandoned the fight. He preferred to keep people alive. Especially pilgrims. If you're in danger, threatened by wild dogs, for example, or thunderstorms. Voilà, there he is to help. Even if you're agnostic. Or Moorish. Even if you don't believe in anything. It's enough to be on a long road. Or in a stone boat. With seagulls at your side. Pity, he counsels. Goodwill. Do I dare?

24.
Pedestals

It's already weird to have—to feel—this… tenderness towards these pedestalized gentlemen. Santiago. Silène. The Christ of Saint Germain de l'Auxerrois. Me, the monstrous dyke who howls like a wolf. Loves to see things break, fall, burn. Imagine the buildings themselves on the ground. Words liberated from books, from pages. Letters liberated from words. Beauty liberated from art. Sound from sense. And children from their families as ordered by Jesus and Engels alike.

But it's true. I love pedestals. You can put anything on top. Without needing to destroy a thing. Time crumbles things by itself. Then you can keep track of empty alcoves, and one day or other install

yourself there like a hermit crab and display yourself for a moment or ten just as you are—half sphinx, half dyke, half spud. It's a charitable act—giving others the chance to respond to normally hidden things. And throw rotten junk at you. To embrace you.

Usually, I speak into the void. I send my columns by email. Never look at comments. Maybe there aren't any. I'm the vapor that's produced when potatoes are at a full boil. I disperse. Cling. Leave only a humid trail on the wall.

This time, I set a timer. These spuds won't burn. At least, I hope. They speak to me. In the beginning they said, "We're hard." After a moment. "Not too." Then, "Not at all." "Shit. It's all over." They were covered in soil. Cheap. Sold by a grey guy who jerked, then winked an eye. Lifted a shoulder up to his ear from time to time. And to me, responded to each demand in bad English. Insisted. Even if I was speaking French correctly, fluently. I have an accent. That's all. So, here's a foreigner. Too bad. So what. Hello? Hello? I don't concede.

—Des champignons, s'il vous plait. (Some mushrooms, please.)

—Another thing?

A nearby vendor shouts to the guy, "You speak Portuguese, too? Ha-ahahahaha."

Fucking asshole. Mind your own business. Your own stall, for that matter.

Fucking spuds. I should have said something. It's not their fault. Poor taters in their hot and innocent bath.

Soft. Sweet. After a life in the dark and silence, they give in to the fork. I'm not that obliging. Am a lot harder. Like the rocks that were their companions. Or not. A real hard case wouldn't be bothered. Not at all. By this nonsense. But today, I'm fragile. Nothingness troubles me. Maybe this encounter was my fault. Maybe I didn't really speak French at all. I opened my mouth and the words fled, are hidden somewhere.

"Who do you think you are? Go back where you came from."

No, not quite yet. I see an empty niche in the palace wall. There's a pedestal somewhere.

Berk

25.
Language

Burn, water. Blow, stone. Break, air. Flow, earth. Why fight for the right to speak? In French, or even English? Adding my voice to the buzz, to people who murmur, cry, babble, invoke. And afterwards do nothing. Or too much. Nothing's simpler than a revolution. The end of the world. An exploding vest. Weight loss. With chimeric words one can create anything, destroy anything. Even lies are stones for people like my mother. You can say that the world is round and they can respond, "No." And that ends that. Logic—useless. Facts, words—powerless. A bee has more weight in her stinger. The body that remains isn't neutral either. Listen…

Yesterday, I tried to call her. And both times, I heard her say, "Hello? Hello?" And me, I shouted, "Mom! Mom! It's Kelly. It's Kenny. It's Kali." She didn't hear anything. A problem of the telephone. The symbolic. Long live metaphors for the language itself which wounds, separates, excludes. Rosemary isn't thyme. And me, if you call me human, I have nothing to do with plants. A total failure.

How words are too light or too dense. They wound. They heal. If, in the silence, I just wanted to say, "Marina," it's too intimate. It hurts, disturbs. I don't dare call to her. Her name will explode like a bomb. "Marina." I touch her. My hand silently asks, "Do you love me?"

Beloved city, country. How can I survive your blows when I just want to enter into your life? Move through the river no collisions, be totally liquid?

26.
Space-Time with Charles-Michael

It becomes possible, even in exile. To have a life that's liquid and light despite the flagrant contradiction of the time-space continuum all in crumbs. The secret—letting everything go. Entering into the agoraphobic space of freedom. That is, the condition of nothingness, of lack. Landmarks—none. You can lose yourself. But you can also get lost clinging to fleeting things. I watch the flight of youth. Of flesh. Various hopes. Social change that never comes according to plan. Or money. Too bad.

Before, long before all that, I spent a week in Paris with my ex, Amy. Each night, we ate together, but that was it. During the day, I wandered alone. The first day, I dared ask for *une café* somewhere, and the guy corrected the gender, « Un, un café ». Afterwards, I didn't step foot into a restaurant or bar. I looked at the grey stones and the river. After two, three days of that, I became mute. Feral, practically. Was filled with mist and rain. Emptied of sound, of sense. Of history. Community. Language. The fire and blood of the world.

It was a kind of death. We humans die a lot. And miraculously resurrect ourselves. With maybe a few pieces less. A toe. An eye. Still, we persist. Ana's brother, Miguel, he persisted to his last breath in a state of freedom. Of perpetual self-invention. Re-birth. Staying with us for his chemo, I was never quite sure who would emerge from his room. Sometimes, it was the little brother of that stinking island, the nice gay Cuban. Other times, it was the big boss, heterosexual and American. Chop, chop. I'm so important. A real bossman. The head!

Everything that was open and sweet in him, everything gay, he dropped and hid in exile. Didn't share with anyone. Not a lesbian colleague. Or his dyke sister, Marina. Coming to us every Thanksgiving, he said he hated labels. He even changed his name. Deny it, and all the pain associated with it would be exiled, too. Well, he succeeded. More or less. Except that, his life fragmented, one chunk at his job, another for his relatives, still others no where, he found himself alone at the end. Isolated. In fact, stuck staying with his horribly out dyke older sister and her girlfriend, whom he barely knew.

Occasionally, at the end, he tried to re-assemble all the bits. One day at the oncologist, he told me a story about a lover. How they'd spent all their days and nights together. Inseparable. Sleeping on the beach just until dawn one silhouette pressed tight to the back of the other. I don't remember the end of the story. A break-up? Work camps? Exile? Death? He lost so many to AIDS. Suicide. Despair. The usual nonsense, right? So… That's why he wanted to bury all that. Deny it. Me, I fled Kentucky. Became a foreigner. I chew off my fingernails. Sometimes even my fingers.

For his vacations, he'd travel to Morocco. Find young handsome guides. That he probably slept with far from home. What did he think about there in our house, stretched out all alone on the empty bed? Then in the hospital? He must have been so afraid, a terrible emptiness and no comfort. No back. No masculine love. None of the body's mysterious tenderness.

27.
Tashlikh

Don't judge. Don't judge. You, too, you've left essential things behind. And you never know which hole will be filled with diamonds, which with mud, or spiderwebs, cigarette butts, words. At any rate, it's too late. There are plants that don't demand to be harvested. Either you look at them and exclaim, "You're so beautiful." Or you toss them out.

Once in Angers, we saw a huge fish on the Maine river. It followed the current, made circles in the water. Had a great, big belly. Had everything, in fact, except life. A fisherman told us that it was a catfish, a poisson-chat. Fish cat. I didn't hear poisson, but poison. Marina, too, because she asked the gentleman if the water wasn't clean? Was it so contaminated that it killed the fish?

"Oh, no," he said. "Everybody thinks that. But the last few years the water is much better. As for me, I eat fish from the river. Of course I do."

And he explained a bunch of other things, too, about global warming. (It wasn't really that bad.) The birds (Have you seen the swans?) The local plants. The city's politicians (that keep him from catching as many fish as he wanted). It was hot. The fisherman stank. I stared at the dead fish. It wasn't that stiff. Not yet. He and the water played. He didn't complain. Flowed like the Seine under the Mirabeau bridge. Like the beer in the Mirbel café. Like bread crumbs tossed in a river. Forgive us.

28.
Persimmon

Or not. We're all lost. Today, I rage. I cling. I sink. I grieve the persimmon tree massacred in the Luxembourg. When I arrived, it was nothing but a stump. Why amputate its arms? Prune the thing in August with its fruits? The last time, it had these little green balls everywhere. It's monstrous. Especially this one. That I've visited for years. A decade at least. This little persimmon, kaki tree that also sprouts in Kentucky hedgerows.

It was my grandmother who showed it to us. We were in the country. It was hot. We were looking for a thorny blackberry thicket, and walked a long time under the sun. The road wasn't paved. I was the littlest. I probably whined. My grandmother stopped occasionally. "Here, taste this." Or. "Don't eat that! You have to wait for the frost." In the city, far from wild gardens, she didn't talk much, just sat in front of the TV. She crocheted. My grandfather didn't talk much either after their flight from the capricious land. We were visiting their relatives. They had finally gotten an indoor toilet at home. In the cellar some aunt had infinite rows of preserves. Outside, the corn was a lot taller than me, and dangerous.

They've been dead a long time, these people. But when I found that persimmon tree in Paris. There in the orchard, its branches all natural and wild among the apple trees and grape vines that were so controlled... It seemed to represent me. I saw myself as family. Felt welcome.

I was obviously wrong. Oh, dear persimmon tree. With your fruits that look like tomatoes, but more orange, with your taste of mango or of peach liberated by frost.

I walk towards the hives. What other disasters might await me? The bees are there. They're in the grass, on the lawn. There are a lot of hives. A sign explains that it's already been done, the honey harvest. And that it was bigger than the two previous years. They'll sell the honey at the end of September.

Silène, also, is in his spot. Still drunk. Still smiling. I find a chair in a sunny corner. The weather is nice for the others. For me, too, I admit. No, I won't deny this little pleasure.

29.
The Art of Losing

I should do some shopping, but I stay at home. It's raining. Yes, it's pouring again in that continuous way. And the humidity and moisture cling to everything. To the walls, the furniture, my hair, our clothes. I shouldn't have done laundry yesterday. But too late. It's there on the drying rack. The tee shirts and socks that are feeding mold.

Fuck.

I'm tired. Depressed.

I read a Scandinavian novel translated into French. It does me good. Nobody's more unhappy than Harry Hole, Norwegian detective and drunk. Even the people who came back from sunny vacations and found themselves under this incessant Parisian rain are happier than him.

I look for an Elizabeth Bishop poem. It's not hard. I always carry around a collection of her poems, like a pink bible. I find it there, *The Fish*. I read it. After weeks of French, her English seems entirely new. With a music, a beauty that are almost shocking. I gasp at each word, each phrase that is so simple and pure. I'm saved. I imagine that that's what it's like to be a poet-genius. That they know how to reinvent language each time they approach the page, giving words back their meanings. Or maybe this magic is mostly rare. Even most of the people who meditate day and night never get to Nirvana. Fisherfolk don't always find their fish.

But Elizabeth Bishop, yes. Orphan, dyke, traveller, lover of trees, the perpetual guest, drunk, she learned to lose, was even an expert in the art. Learning, she wrote, "isn't hard to master." Though that was a lie. No, not a lie, a kind of joke. She never mastered anything but poetry, where she revealed herself by hiding. Put her pain in boxes of polished words. I do it, too. Not as well as her. But I have my little square chapters. My essays. The boxes that linger in Valerie's cellar. How many times have I left? From how many places?

Once, when I was a student, I went to a farm with some friends. It had a wooded part with the skeletons of cows who chose that place to die. Their ribs were the vaults of a church. You can't go further than that—death. At dusk, I lit a fire. I was a Girl Scout as a kid. We painted our faces. I murmured a kind of prayer in Spanish, which was just like Latin.

The trees were so dark. We heard rustling everywhere under the moon. Little animals. The earth. We probably drank—and smoked. Maybe took acid. I don't remember anymore. We were filled with night, the darkness, peace. Near midnight, we decided to head for the cars. In the meadow, we heard the rumble of thunder. Felt the earth quake. "Quick, to the gate!" It was a stampede, a river of enormous and magnificent beasts with no mercy in them for life.

T'es sale!

30.
The Shower

I was wrong. Apparently, I, too, have memories. A toe in that collective, continuous river of Mnemosyne that lives above all in jokes, in banter, stories told around our holiday tables. In the photos on the wall. In our bodies.

"She has her aunt's eyes. What was she called? The one who died in Illinois?"

This week, Marina's in Angers with her family where her face finds its echoes in theirs. I avoid the bed which is so big, so cold, and terribly empty. And I walk. I walk, I read, I watch *Sœur Thérèse dot com* online because our TV is on strike. I also jot down here that I ate all the grub at home. Including the canned cassoulet. The chocolate with hazelnuts. The crackers. The cheese. Soup and popcorn, too. I also drank some wine, the little bit that was left. Instant coffee—my mother's favorite. And a can of beer—Pelforth brune, which I adore. I devoured some frozen veg as well. What else? My fingernails. And cuticles.

I go to the Bastille market with bloody hands, looking for the churros guy. He's not there. I look at everything there is. But can't bring myself to ask for anything. Even if the prices are good. The stuff is beautiful. And I'm so hungry.

I think I recognize a woman, a famous American poet. We met in Cincinnati. I flee, terrified. At the last moment I buy several apples. A lot. I eat one. Then another. Then a third. There's juice everywhere. Crumbs. Stains. Actually, I should take a bath. I should have done it yesterday. I'll do it right now. But first, my email. Then, another apple. A kebab sandwich with fries. There's no more chocolate. But I find some raisins. The bathroom awaits. It's cold in there. Even in August here, we're cold. Besides, there's a really large mirror, a reminder I'm not at all a spirit, but a real person, solid. Of flesh and blood. These chubby legs are mine. Along with my mom's bony chest. And a skin that speaks. Of origins and privilege. Of age. No, I'm not young anymore. And look at my stance. That dykely slouch. Those clothes. There's definitely too much information that anybody at all can read. I'm so vulnerable and there's no reinforcements on the way.

I should have gone with Marina. I need her voice. Her presence. Her body. Our life, as they say, in common. I wanted to write these four days without distractions, with the apartment and the city all to myself. But I haven't left the starting block. It's my fault. I don't want to give myself as completely as before. I don't want to be hurt. We're going to leave soon.

And yet, and yet. I open the door.

I take off my clothes.

31.
The Train to Angers

This time I'm not going for good. I'm headed to Angers where Ana's with her mother. The guy next to me stinks. He should take a bath occasionally, I think. Yes, I'm a hypocrite. Too bad. The landscape that passes is so flat and empty you could see a dog. A marmot. A cow pie. A fly on the horizon. Now, there's corn along the tracks. And some unknown thing with little flowers. I'm facing backwards. Am about to puke. The white windmills do their elegant dance.

I imagine myself in a painting of that almost autumnal field. Smell the perfume of the earth. Animals. My boots are full of mud. The sun beats down. There's also straw beneath my feet. A little further, there are huge trees. The sky is not a dark January blue, or the light blue of August. But between the two. There are a couple of clouds. In the distance, I see a house, but it's not mine. So no need for details.

What am I wearing aside from muddy boots? Black pants? An almost purple tee-shirt? City clothes. I have my backpack, too. With my computer inside and paperwork that I should have filled out ages ago. What am I doing in the mud? Is it a film? Is this research? I think I'm not doing anything. I'm just there, that's it. Somebody's gonna come with their John Deere tractor and plow me into the earth. I'll become part of it. Disappear. Ten years later. Or a thousand. They'll find fragments of my bag with bits of plastic and metal from my laptop. My bones will be clean. Liberated from flesh and from feeling. From fear. Nostalgia which is as paralyzing and destructive as cancer. Hate also remains behind to feed the grass. The animals. Or hold up, maybe, the next suburb.

I imagine you, too, inside the passing train. You look at me for a moment. Remain silent. Don't join me.

you think
youre going
somewhere?

32.
Rue de la Parcheminerie, Angers

I arrive. The door opens and Marina smiles at me. She is beautiful. Her eyes are extra green and happy because of me. It's incredible. That I can inspire such a thing. I feel shy. But after a moment, I smile, too, am so happy. I'd forgotten. I'm not all alone in the world.

She tells me to hide a minute in the bedroom.

"Who's that?" asks her mother, Faustina.

"Nobody. Let's continue." They were exercising.

After a moment, I enter.

"Surprise!" I don't shout too loud. I'm afraid of giving her a heart attack.

Faustina laughs. Is pleased. They keep working for a few more minutes. I hear their voices. They are speaking Spanish. I've heard it for twenty years, more, really. My Pavlovian response changes frequently. Marina and I speak English together. Often, Spanish on the telephone is a sign of imminent trouble, illnesses, accidents, bad news. But sometimes, during vacations, holidays like Christmas with her family, it's the language of community, neighborhood, belonging. It creates mysterious ties. And this time, after a month of French, I'm happy to hear it.

I learned it in school, beginning in the second grade. Yes, there in Kentucky. It was astonishing that a chair could also be called *silla*.

I didn't really believe that somewhere, people spoke it all the time. No, it was some secret thing. And that was really handy. When I started keeping a diary I wrote it in Spanish. My mother who rummaged through all our stuff like a cop or a priest looking for sin didn't have any way to read it. In a desperate attempt to express herself safely, one of my sisters actually wrote on the underside of furniture, *I hate my mother*.

Mom didn't find that phrase until recently under a hidden corner of her desk. She wept, asked me if I'd done it. But no. I didn't need to. I had this foreign language. I confided my poems to it. Prayers. Desires—both suicidal and murderous. Missing? The ideas, the desires so unthinkable they didn't even cross my mind.

33.
Notebooks

Poor girl with her notebooks in broken, basic Spanish. I should feel sorry for her, but I'm doing the same thing, right? Or almost. Here in French. Besides, she learned some important things. It's already a big deal to figure out that things have many names. Pseudonyms. And secret names still unknown. Even me, I have others. A Spanish teacher called me Queli. I really liked the Aztec flavor. Me llama Queli Coatl. Here in France, they call me a range of things. Caler Bogswell. Fally Gogswell. Names, people, gender are so changeable.

Back in Kentucky, I knew this one girl and her brother from Guatemala. We spoke Spanish together. She had this long, dark, beautiful hair, was on my field hockey team. Her brother liked me. But I liked his sister. We were all happier in Spanish, set apart. In fact, *una silla* is not a chair. When I speak French, I can be cute as anything, or oddly authoritarian. The language evokes whatever it will. Once, their whole family came over to my house. I had a tumor on my leg. Nothing serious, but there was an operation scheduled. They prayed in Spanish and anointed my leg with a glistening oil. Nothing happened, or disappeared. My friends were mortified. Afterwards, we never referred to it again. Either in English or Spanish.

When I got to New York in 1989, I found out that everybody spoke Spanish. At least 1.87 million people, practically a third of the town. It was really useful in the modest, Spanish neighborhoods where I lived, but the language wasn't magical anymore. Doesn't matter. I didn't need to hide notebooks or feelings. I came out. I could speak directly. Say yes. Say no. I could offer my chest. My heart. Poems to everyone like everybody. Sadly, even at a cut-rate price it was hard to unload them. There was already a glut on the market.

Now, I have another language. Another notebook. I write, *tu*, you. I write *toi*. I imagine you. I pursue you. This is not a game.

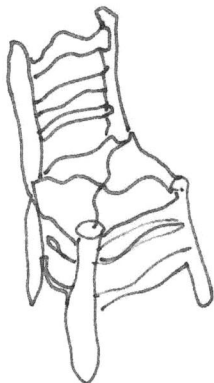

34.
The Nest, Angers

Here, among family, in Spanish, I don't talk much. Like a good immigrant, I do things. Cook. Assemble Ikea furniture. A bedside table. Shelves. I take care of people, too. When she was still in New York, it was me who took care of Faustina's wound when she fell and cracked her skull like a poor hard-boiled egg. For Miguel, when he was hungry, I made picadillo, and lamb and apricot tagine.

It's enough. These gestures in the world of things. Of flesh. I'm such a good son-in-law, daughter-in-law. I always nod my head. Feel comfortable. Feel so stupid, so foreign. Shit, let it go. They always welcome me. Faustina even forgets I'm not from Cuba. I know all the names, the places, the characters. The secrets. How much mothers hate their daughters' freedom. How they complain. Denounce. To preachers. Why not the security forces? That toss them in jail, or worse. Forget about it. Just stop.

Here in Angers, she's happy enough. Has her own room. Her son. People that come to visit speak Spanish or English. She didn't go that far. Not far at all. She has her words. People know her story. Except the shameful bits. (Let it go. She's not the enemy anymore. Have pity on her.)

Except that it's not true she's known. This figure has become Luis' mother. A generic old lady. Not at all Faustina. Her life, even as a young girl, is hidden behind wrinkles. White hair. An empty, emptied smile. She's not there any more. She who wanted to be a doctor, was a teacher. She travels all the time. From one minute to the next, she's in another space-time. Parallel. Or perpendicular. Dunno. Someone speaks to her. She fights to return, stay. She pauses, stops. Resumes. Has become something else in this city of grey roofs. Brick chimneys. Antennas. She looks at the cat across the street, and the cathedral with its two spires just there, behind. Then she falls asleep in her chair. A little further away is the Maine river and its befouled fish. At night, in the little narrow streets, with solid stones, students and drunks scream their heads off. Without her hearing aids, Faustina doesn't hear anything. Is happy. Sleeps well in her nest.

No, she's not happy either. Nor that word, content, which evokes a stale baguette. It's more that Faustina is tired. Vanquished. After Miguel's death she submitted. Doesn't have the right anymore to stuff herself with candy and ice cream. In any case, not every day. Even if, like me, her last remaining passion is eating. Like me. She expresses herself with it. Is starving.

What else is there to do? Cry, rage, scratch, and then? You eat. Love. Why do I always forget about that? We're not at home. But we're together. In the same boat there at the Luxembourg. Pushed by children. Rented by the half-hour. And together we persist.

Fluctuat nec mergitur. Rocked by the waves, but still afloat.

35.
Bonkers, the Nostalgic Boar

We came back yesterday. The train got into Paris forty minutes late. A boar, a metaphor, was on the tracks somewhere. Dead or alive, dunno. Rue Daubenton, we found chestnut leaves already on the sidewalk. The summer fled. Two months already in this apartment. I haven't burnt or broken anything lately. It doesn't bother me anymore how people look at me. The buildings and the stones are less heavy. The foreignity dissolves. I speak if I need to. With or without an accent. It doesn't matter.

Except that, it's still not like it was before. I'm less sensitive. I see, I sense so little when I walk in the streets. Well, I still smell bread. I'm always alert to food. I begin to believe I'd imagined the connection to this place, this city that had been so strong before that I practically died when I left. No, it never existed. Or wasn't all that strong. I wonder if I'm the victim of nostalgia. Of declaring that everything was better before. Or elsewhere. You shouldn't swim, drown in memories, old photos. Still, I look at a couple. At 12, my face smooth. Eyes filled with God. I had a nice smile at 16 when I took handfuls of random pills. Sometime in high school. Behind me, the tree I used to climb.

My mother often looked at her own snapshots. She said, "Oh, that dress was so beautiful." "I was so happy." "I should never have gotten married, had you kids."

She was so sure she would have stayed happy. I'm not sure she ever was. Her favorite photo was taken at a brief, fleeting moment at a party. Even if she was, full of joy, being an unmarried secretary at fifty, at sixty…? A woman like her, who made fun of old maids? No, that would be total failure. The sea-green silk flows around her, burns.

As for Marina and I, we eat pasta. Watch soccer. 1-1. Let the present impose itself. Today, at least. I listen to the cars and the students. I hear my heart beat, beat, beat. I feel the fecal matter that makes its little trip of 7.5 meters. I walk. I look. I walk faster and faster. Some lady on the sidewalk makes fun of me, and shouts, "Un, deux, un, deux !" She has grey, greasy hair. She stinks. "One, two. One, two." And snickers.

It's nice out. It is, it always will be, sunny. Always 1 p.m. No, 1:01. 1:02. Actually, it would be nice to have a two-part face that could look behind and ahead. The future, the past. The supra present. Wait! I'm talking too much. Breathe. Relax. The sun! The sun! Heart! Blood which flows! Eyes! Hair which grows!

I recoil in front of the void, forgetfulness. Death. She comes sooner or later. She takes it all.

36.
The Plague

There's an epidemic in Paris. I've seen it. Epicenter—Rue Abel Hovelacque. It's not deadly, but you still have to pay attention. I've tripped several times. Have even fallen. They emerge from the sidewalk. These tarry mounds. Little pestilential hills. Often grapefruit-sized. Or mandarinish. I've seen them in groups of five or six. Sometimes alone. Why do they exist, these little tits? Is there hunger in the neighborhood? Is it a mute protest of subjugated women? Maybe there are stony puppies, rocky kids that wait somewhere in the neighborhood.

I've seen others elsewhere, too. And traces of mastectomies. Done, I suppose, without anesthesia. The groans of the sidewalk passing unnoticed by the neighbors. Have you heard them, seen these apparitions? Or the scars that are lighter than the flat, grey, empty chests of the sidewalks? I doubt it. People don't see anything. Even if

they fall. It's just some kind of irregularity. You get up. Keep going with a slightly bloody knee when you should stay on the ground. Should suck, be nourished by this ultra unexpected gift.

Better think about it. Maybe I should paint them. Yeah, a pretty beige. With a dark brown nipple. You have to be absolutely narrative about it. Nobody gets the subtle, the abstract. Maybe the kids even of concrete haven't seen a thing. Are dying of hunger somewhere. In corners. With bits of gravel. I'd really like to know who, what these nipples are for. And to see the little creatures grow-up. Run through the streets. Like boar. Or crocodiles. Armadillos. Elephants. All wild. All hard.

They aren't like most statues. Born like Athena. Sprung from a skull cracked and often nourished by words. Ideas. Marianne, at the Place de la République, she embodies something totally precise. Further along, at the Place de la Nation she has a sister mistreated by taggers. This Republic has as companions the Genius of Liberty, Justice and Equality, Work, Learning, Abundance and Wealth. They grew inside Jules Dalou's head when he was in exile. Finally back at home, Dalou was lighter, more free, could sculpt my friend at the Luxembourg, the drunk dreamer Silène.

But these others. I'd be thrilled and terrified to see them run wild through the street. Me, made mostly of water. Empty space. With minerals, too, but less than necessary. Mine, my tits. They're all soft. With me they nourish only pleasure. Outside, are signals, targets. These two mysterious things that join me, or separate me from others. Tomorrow, I'll come back. Paint. Find a hidden corner, and wait. That's what the lions do in Africa. They wait for their prey at waterholes. Maybe they only come out at night. Maybe at dawn. I'll be there.

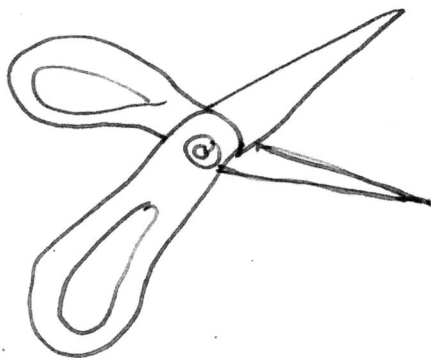

37.
The Cut

Yeah, I'll be there. So squishy. Monstrous. Unstable. With nails that grow all the time without stopping. And break, hiding things. Hair is even worse. I never stay the same. Transform as if I were a, a what? A flower? An insect? Something mythical. Humans, even gods don't become minerals, but animals. Sometimes plants. Like Swan-Zeus who raped Leda, knocked her up with two little chicks. Did they prefer corn or milk? They at least had human mugs. Helen's the most beautiful of all.

Me, I'm more froggish. Look at the photos. I've changed so much. Size. Hair. You know, I was an egg, a fish. Either I stay a little more myself—the branch grafted to the tree—or become something even more radical. Yesterday, I went to the hairdresser. Her sister who was shampooing my hair, accused me, "You have dandruff."

"Oh, yes?" I wondered if I was becoming something else. A serpent-woman shedding her skin.

"Really a lot!" She exclaimed. She waited for some response from me. An expression of shame? Or horror?

"The pool," I said. "The chemicals. It's no big deal."

She made a sound and said something to her sister in a Chinese language. She should have been more patient. They, too, are becoming something else. Not trees or birds, but they speak French with their clients. I've seen their mother. They don't walk like her anymore. Have their hair in another style. On their faces, they wear foreign expressions. They won't notice to what point they've changed until they go back to China. When their aunts are maybe horrified at these two French girls.

The sister scratches at my head with her fingernails. Tries to remove the dandruff, and the scalp with it. Maybe even my skull. Trying to discover if I have something inside.

Careful, Lady. It's dangerous, putting your hands in my head. Since I was thirteen I've been waiting for an explosion that's quick, bloody, deadly. And cerebral, of course.

38.
Alien

Or from the chest. Dunno. Barely teens, my sisters and I walked to the movie house through suburban streets. First they were long, with little separated houses. Tiny yards. Extreme boredom. Silence. And heat. Then there was a big, ugly, dangerous street that took us to a concrete-block building.

I thought it was wonderful and mysterious. My grandfather worked there for a while as a ticket taker after his life on the farm and in the factory. We used to see all the Walt Disney films for free. This time, my sisters chose a totally different kind of thing. And I screamed from the moment the baby alien attached itself to the face of some poor unlucky fuck. It was like a detached hand, an untamed lobster. Almost immediately another sprang from the chest or the stomach in an impressive flow of blood. I screamed again, and kept my eyes more or less closed until the end. Especially when the big one came. I peeked, saw the half-human, half-roach monster with its long, armored limbs.

I was terrified. What foreignness. What rage. Faced with it, the poor children of apes with their own soft, mushy bodies. Not at all practical for deep space. Or even the terrors of earth aside from snakes, and spiders which in my childhood didn't bother me at all. At night, I could venture down to our basement which was so dark my sisters refused to go. Hell held no terror when I had God. Still though, I was still terrified by the cinematic attacks of ants. Or bees. Or birds. Maybe because they changed the laws of nature. Signaled the artifice of the known universe. Or the unrelenting, mutual hate between the creatures which emerge from cracks or do unexpected things, and… all the rest. Like me.

Even if I hadn't yet understood my strangitude. Believed that my sisters were the aliens. From a planet full of tears and of boys. Smokes and make-up. Just like my mother, even more furious and bloody than them.

Greetings
Earthlings

114

39.
The Return

Now, I'm the extraterrestrial. Especially there in the United States where I should feel at home. And sometimes, I am. Maybe surrounded by other homos. Other activists or artists as kinly strange in the world as me. But then the weather changes. Political sands shift. I wake up to the clanging of a bell. Targeted by hate or fear, as bad as extreme solicitude, and I become foreign, alien, lost.

I eat despair with my two croissants. This fucking French I write in, this broken world. Marina goes to the swimming pool. Returns. It was closed. Marina and I, then, will take a little walk. We go down the staircase with its soft, worn carpet. Outside, something has changed. The sidewalks are less deserted. And the street is filled with cars. They vomit out people and their things. Suitcases. Backpacks. Little animals and humans. They cry out. They take their place among the dried leaves on the sidewalk. The city is happy. My beloved. She takes pleasure in her inhabitant ants.

We walk. With steps that are a little more energetic. The store at the corner is open for the first time this month. And all the cafés. At the Pantheon, there are students. With their notebooks. Dirty messy hair. The cultivated air of neglect. Their heads elsewhere. In philosophy, politics. Ideas. Words. Dare I say—art. It doesn't matter if it's a pose. It helps me. And me, I feel something. Something dangerous. An opening.

I see the buildings as more beautiful. More... awake. We don't take our usual routes. I begin to remember why I wanted to come back. Why I was happy here among these old, worn stones. The places that speak. The statues. The pebbles. Yes, I know I have a place. And words, too, even fugitive, fleeting. The theater, there, is ours, all of us who persist. I warn you. I'm inside this river. I will give you everything. Time. The city. I am hers. Among the dead and the living, arm in arm. Behind me, threads of music. Everything is bright and luminous. Blessed.

40.
Saint Geneviève

To get that feeling back, of being at home. In this world of stone, of deaths, of light. It's a gift. A curse. I'll have to leave again. It's not a big deal. I'll live. Even if I complain, cry, find everything horrible and dark. I'll get over it. I've done it before. I'll do it again, always. I hope.

I feel so good, that even later, when we walk along Rue de la Montagne Sainte-Geneviève right to the church Saint-Étienne-du-Mont I'm not annoyed that it's not hers, not at all, the site of Saint Geneviève's grave, now protector of beautiful Lutetia. Still, she was there. Still, we went in. We stayed. Breathed the perfume of old wood, incense, stone. Everything is mine. Nothing.

Even if it was the hour for mass. And inside, in this vast church a priest in front of a little group of women. I was afraid. A little. They were my mother, my sister. They hated me. They loved me. Were so calm, so tranquil in their little community where they could be more than an insignificant body. A machine for work. Mothers. Spouses. And where they discovered the pleasure of belief as rigid and firm and fixed as the firmaments. They don't build churches from nothing. From paper and string. Like my sphinx wings. Oh God and his stupidities. These mammals trapped by the impressive speed of fear. Of love.

I wonder if some were in the street for the big demonstration *Manif pour Tous* terrified by the idea of my homo marriage. If they believe I could destroy their families, the State itself. If they knew that this deluge of hate resulted in wounds, the death of people like us, Marina and me. Yes, I wonder.

Behind them, in front. I'm invisible. Sad.

But for the moment, I'm not afraid of their certitudes as hard as stone, as knives because Saint Genevieve is there, protector of the city, and of us, her pedestrian-dykes, her citizens in love.

41.
The Scale

I make breakfast. Oatmeal. Coffee. And I see some-thing unexpected on my ankle. It shines. What is that? Glinting purple and green?

I touch it. Wonder what I'm becoming this time. Maybe I'll be a mermaid. A real one. Is it a gift or a trap? Caught, as always between lands and seas. Everything would be open to me, thus nothing. The normal exilian state. Shouldn't be so pessimistic. I could learn to love the ocean's chill, the heat of shores. Water and rocks both. Maybe this strange and aging body will become entirely supple, entirely smooth. Mythic and young.

Old fish, as for them, with their skin of scales, they don't have wrinkles. Don't become dried up, diminished. They actually get bigger. Become more resolute. Capable perhaps of plunging to the depths of things. Mermaids sing, too. Not with voices as deep as whales. But they sing. They swim. And they seduce fisher(wo)men. Some-times they save them.

I already hear the first beautiful notes. Yesterday, we ate sardines. Hence my future in the shining scale that remains. It multiplies, colonizes my knees. Legs. Belly. Once, I saved a girlfriend from drowning. Her father was a preacher. He was happy I was baptized. She wanted to learn to swim. Had already taking swimming lessons, but was afraid. One August night, we went down to the pool. She began to swim in the water that was so cold, so silent. Reassured, she ventured into a deeper part. And immediately panicked. Struggled. Sank. I grabbed her, drug her to the edge of the pool. She hung on, breathed, laughed. Kissed me for a long time. Then she did it all over again.

The deep water. The panic. The rescue. The kiss. Afterwards, she told me that the Chinese believed that if you saved someone's life, you were responsible for it forever. I didn't know. Not long after, I took the bus to New York.

As for Marina, she swims really well. Her mother, too.

42.
Heritage Day

The French, alas, don't swim as well as they should. At best, they just scrape by. Today, they're outside in the sun for French Heritage Day. They look at the installations of giant photos featuring men in their hats, and women in dresses and ugly shoes who are nevertheless victorious against the Krauts. They visit City Hall, Notre Dame. Monumental Paris. But also the sewers, the catacombs. Searching for their own threads. An entry. An exit. I look at them with tenderness.

Especially those with Gauls as ancestors. They seem so anxious. They panic. Cling. Suspect that aside from their factories, it's their history that's disappearing in an absolute sense. It's true. That's the nature of Time. Even soldiers, the aging citizens who were there for the Liberation, have moved too much. Can't go back. The language that you also think you have is ripped away. Each new generation re-seasons the words, each hungry mouth. My girlfriend, French citizen of Cuban origin. Me, who has wandered through these streets obsessed by the voids and pedestals of the city. And the other French people, those with roots elsewhere, they also look for ties. Maybe hold dear ideas that are always more glorious than reality. Marina and I, also, love liberty, equality, fraternity, but above all the elusive laïcité which allows us the hope, as women, as dykes that we'll get the rest some day.

Once again, we visit the church St. Germain de l'Auxerrois where I put my fingers in the water. It's cold, clean. I raise my hand, just a little. I stop short. Ask myself if I'm really going to make that gesture. The sign of the cross. Am I nuts or what? No. I just wanted the feeling, yes, of believing. Of entering for the last time into that sacred space, of belonging.

It's not only churches. The other day, I went to a bookstore looking for connections. It was a dyke event. I didn't stand out at all among these women. Often with really short hair. Calm, open faces which were mostly white. But even there, I wasn't at home. I brought the scent of distant fields and of trains. Metros with their industrial soap and pools of piss. I should have taken a bath.

And I saw the nets. The ties between them all that excluded me but also trapped them. Old friendships. Old loves. Hates, maybe. You could see diplomas, too. And I didn't say anything to anybody. Stayed standing in the back of the room with another girl with blue streaks in her hair. And a stressed out face. Who wasn't born among them either. But in a totally different group. Of men. But she wanted to belong to this one. Like me. Nevertheless. And yet. Make do, we must.

43.
No, No, Victor Hugo

It seems really late, too late. To become one with any-thing. A community. A god. A state. Any language at all. I don't have my childhood accent anymore. Have forgotten my grandmother's homey sayings. What good is it to keep my pockets filled with pebbles, and buckeyes, arrowheads, flowers? My big speeches will be deep in the woods. In the bathroom. "My fellow citizens." "My beloved…" "Fraternity!" No, I wipe my moist hand on my shirt and flee.

In the street, a generous wino shouts, "Hey, lesbian! Yeah, lesbian. Don't be afraid. I'm not mocking you. Re-ally. I love lesbians. I admire you…" At dinner, a friend makes fun of me when I misgender the word for mus-sels, turning it into something else. "She's going to eat a mold? Ha, ha! It's 'une' moule. Une!"

No, I know exactly who (and what) I am. Belly Hog-swell. Dyke, foreigner. I watch TV. I read. Cry. I eat a salad of fennel in memory of the faggots burned yonks ago in Italy. And for the others, their throats slit, slaughtered, tossed out windows, I sprout wings. They are calm and motionless. Don't act. I reveal my breasts of stone. I take up space. My knees bleed. I am a strange and beautiful sphinx. Who wants nothing.

44.
Last Call, Parents

I talked to my parents yesterday. My father first. He confided to me, "I'm a lot more with it than people think." His voice as beige and placid as he. He didn't tell me how he wrecked the car. Was in the hospital. No, he was absolutely perfect. Even if he didn't play golf anymore. Practically couldn't walk. In the background, I heard the voice of his wife, Susan, spouse #2. She's a nice woman. And thankfully younger than him. They have a grown-up daughter. He's not alone like my mother. My mother with her hesitant, raucous voice. A lot more bird than me.

As for her, she's going to move. Not exactly to a nursing home, but there will be help. "I won't be alone, or have to cook. Not bad, huh?" She tries to laugh. She can take a few things with her. The rest she'll have to sell. Get rid of. Even the canvases that she painted herself, a little Cézannesque, a little Fauve.

When I asked for one, she said, "You have to talk to your cousin. She's the one organizing everything."

Who was this woman? My mother—she preferred being alone. Didn't like anybody. Was furious. Refused every consolation but God. Was vulnerable, yes, fragile, but of stone. Never relinquished control. Never. I wondered if she was preparing to die. Had already done it. And then? With what, how, does one fill the cracks? Would I have the right of return?

45.
And Then, Shit!

Drink champagne, that'll do it. Even in crappy glasses. And eat cod brandade and bread. Olives. Speak French with the others in the menagerie with a terrifying mix of accents. Woof. Woof. Quack, quack. Baaaaaaaa. It's a joy, yes, a joy, an equilibrium. To be here together. All chattering.

And me. I become someone else. Someone happier. Smiling. Clever. Not well-behaved at all. We laugh. We laugh. We laugh. Cock-a-doodle-doo! We're practically ridiculous. You know that joke? Knock-knock. Who's there? Ooops. No. That's not the right one. So, once, there was this French guy, an Italian, an American and Cuban. They walk into a bar, not a bar, but this room, and the Italian said... I don't remember anymore, but something. It doesn't matter...

They lived happily ever after and had a bunch of children. No. No kids either. And there was nothing eternal about it. Nevertheless, they had a very nice evening. Far from their birth countries. And their families. And in this other dimension, there in Paris, or anywhere, really, where glasses are full and words shared they established another republic. Where poets and dykes and fags and trannies are all blessed. Where you can be different, but this difference doesn't weigh too much. And there's no voice which dominates. Or people who feel so at home they plant their flag in your heart and defend it. Oink, oink.

And they lived happily… until the next day when two of the girls took a métro, two trains, then a boat, putting an end to, for the moment, their bipolar lives abroad.

Aquatic Coda

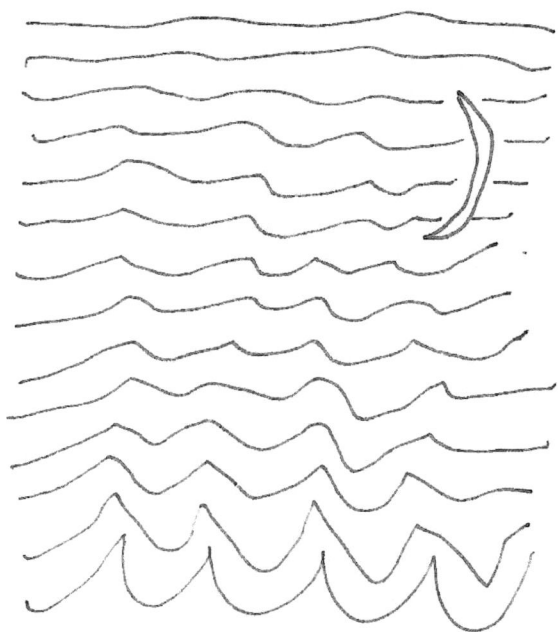

46.
The Boat

I'm in a boat. The sea is a vast plain, grey and beautiful. You can't escape. There's nothing human outside. There's the surface of the water, then the air. Then the sky. What is it called? That place, the interstice where the air all around us becomes sky? Is it a question of distance? At three meters, six, we say air? But at thirteen, three hundred, that is sky? If it moves, we call it something else entirely, wind. Me, too, I have a multitude of names. I nevertheless come when you call.

Over here, there, the air is water. We pass through veils of rain. They erase the division between ocean and air. Everything is soft. Everything is together, unified, One. Except me, this boat. Even if I try to enter the landscape again. If I throw myself in the water and the boat continues, and if I become a part of the horizon. And if I stay there as long as possible. Even if I do that, I'll never be part of the grey sky. Or of water. Too much red inside.

Bones.

And even if I could. If I learned to abandon this skin, and this body of pure water. Release the minerals, the traces, the crumbs of earth, even my names... Or if I become that bird there. Not a chick but a seagull. The almost last. If I fly, and cry and cry. A companion of the water and the air. Then...?

47.
Rain

Dunno. Don't know either how to get all the way to the end. Let things go. I should have. I wanted to stop sooner. With the fairytale about the little party. The dream of love. Of friendship. Refuge. But even there, we're targeted, betrayed. Slaughtered like Huguenots in our most sacred places. Churches. Cafés. Clubs. Yesterday, last week, last year, always. Twenty-three burned alive in New Orleans (1973), the little bomb in New York (1990), in Atlanta (1997). And the massacre at Pulse of course, in Orlando, a couple of days, a couple of decades ago. Pulse. You've already forgotten. And why not? We often find ourselves on bloody floors. In garbage bins, one by one by one. Our bodies which are so horribly tender. So nude. And terrifying. Look! An arm here, there. The hand of Adam and the hand of God in a hot and desperately red ocean. I can't deal with it anymore.

There's a light blue net in the air. The boat is a stain in the ocean which is implacable and virtuous. Vitreous. You, Lutetia, where are you? Your light? Your stones? Your rottening language become first crumbs, then dust. Ashes. At night, I cast them on the sea.

Voilà! In the water, little sparks of extinguished stars. Look. Look. Black holes. They stagger. Weave. They dance again. I love you, you the lights, my lost children. I see you in the water. Brought down, you'll never again return. What would you recount about the so cold, so blue depths? Forget? Forget? Should I take vengeance like the exiled Medea, rejected stranger? Fight fire with fire?

Your children burn.

48.
Seraphim

I'm waiting for a sign. You owe me that, at the very least, dear reader. My chorus as mute and complicit as me. What are we going to do?

Look! Look!

It's a pod of whales. I've never seen them up close. Nearly believed I'd invented them. What bulk. These forms which are enormous and majestic. Ferocious. Who sing. I think they are angels. An interplanetary choir. They—wingless—fly. In the house of God. Are the holy of holies. Will I be invited to join them? Or sent away? Persist. Persist.

They shoot water into the air. They play. They sing. Songs of joy. Of the sun. The marvelous rain, and the beautiful Isabella Rossellini just as fine as a guy or a woman. Italian, French, New Yorker. Spider, bee, Anisoptera. Mary or Athena. Saint Genevieve.

Oh, my goddess of the light-colored eyes. Protector of cities and of people who go out to battle or who return. You who sprang from the head of your father with a spear in your hand. Shake the earth. Upturn the purple waters of the sea. Oh, give us, we who remain, a lucky fate and happiness, soft winds and strong for our voyage without end.

Amen. Amen. Amen.

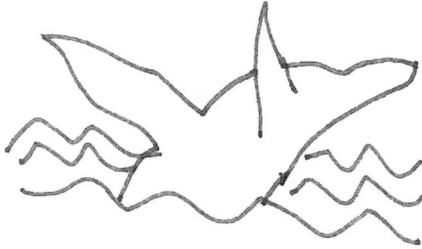

49.
Kyrielle

For the 49 dead
in the anti-gay massacre at Pulse
12 June 2016, Orlando, Florida

Edward Sotomayor Jr., 34
Stanley Almodovar III, 23
Luis Omar Ocasio-Capo, 20
Juan Ramon Guerroro, 22
Eric Ivan Ortiz-Rivera, 36
Peter O. Gonzalez-Cruz, 22
Luis S. Vielma, 22
Kimberly Morris, 37
Eddie Jamoldroy Justice, 30
Darryl Roman Burt II, 29
Deonka Deidra Drayton, 32
Alejandro Barrios Martinez, 21

Anthony Luis Laureano Disla, 25
Jean Carlos Mendez Perez, 35
Franky Jimmy Dejesus Velazquez, 50
Amanda Alvear, 25
Martin Benitez Torres, 33
Luis Daniel Wilson-Leon, 37
Mercedez Marisol Flores, 26
Xavier Emmanuel Serrano Rosado, 35
Gilberto Ramon Silva Menendez, 25
Simon Adrian Carrillo Fernandez, 31
Oscar A. Aracena-Montero, 26
Enrique L. Rios Jr., 25
Miguel Angel Honorato, 30
Javier Jorge-Reyes, 40
Joel Rayon Paniagua, 32
Jason Benjamin Josaphat, 19
Cory James Connell, 21
Juan P. Rivera Velazquez, 37
Luis Daniel Conde, 39
Shane Evan Tomlinson, 33
Juan Chevez-Martinez, 25
Jerald Arthur Wright, 31
Leroy Valentin Fernandez, 25
Tevin Eugene Crosby, 25
Jonathan Antonio Camuy Vega, 24
Jean C. Nives Rodriguez, 27
Rodolfo Ayala-Ayala, 33
Brenda Lee Marquez McCool, 49
Yilmary Rodriguez Sulivan, 24
Christopher Andrew Leinonen, 32
Angel L. Candelario-Padro, 28

Frank Hernandez, 27
Paul Terrell Henry, 41
Antonio Davon Brown, 29
Christopher Joseph Sanfeliz, 24
Akyra Monet Murray, 18
Geraldo A. Ortiz-Jimenez, 25

About the Author

Recognized on several occasions by the New York Press Association, Kelly Cogswell is a prize-winning journalist, essayist, memoirist, and extremely underground artist.

The *Odysseys of Fally Dogswell*, a mediation on language and exile in all its forms, follows her first book, *Eating Fire: My Life as a Lesbian Avenger,* in a trilogy of memoirs.

She lives in Paris.

www.ingramcontent.com/pod-product-compliance
Lightning Source LLC
Chambersburg PA
CBHW051255020426
42333CB00025B/3216